COMIC BOOK SERIES

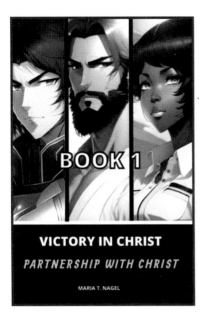

VICTORY IN CHRIST

PARTNERSHIP WITH CHRIST

MARIA T. NAGEL

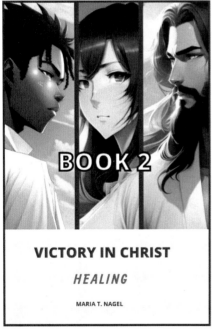

VICTORY IN CHRIST

HEALING

MARIA T. NAGEL

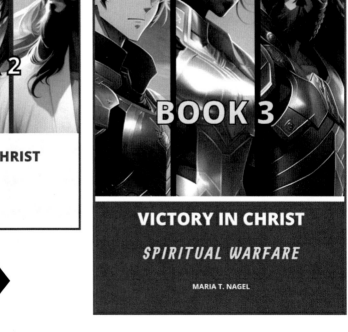

VICTORY IN CHRIST

SPIRITUAL WARFARE

MARIA T. NAGEL

THE AFRICA & DIASPORA EDITION

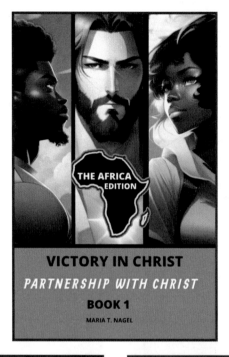

VICTORY IN CHRIST

PARTNERSHIP WITH CHRIST

BOOK 1

MARIA T. NAGEL

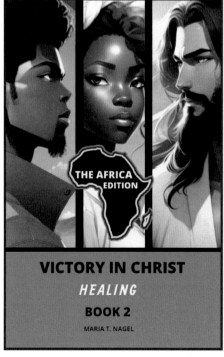

VICTORY IN CHRIST

HEALING

BOOK 2

MARIA T. NAGEL

VICTORY IN CHRIST

SPIRITUAL WARFARE

BOOK 3

MARIA T. NAGEL

FOR WOMEN & TEEN GIRLS

SCAN ME

**SCAN THIS QR CODE
FOR DIRECT ACCESS
TO THE AMAZON REVIEW PAGE**

SHARE YOUR EXPERIENCE
If you enjoyed
our coloring book
we would love to see pictures
and videos of your creations.

Table of Contents

WHO IS
JESUS CHRIST?

The Creator of the universe exists as three divine persons:

God the Father
God the Son, Jesus Christ and
God the Holy Spirit.

2

To provide a simpler explanation, let us consider a triangle.

A triangle is a geometrical figure with three angles.

One shape.
Three sides.

It is similar with God.

There is one God, existing as three divine persons.

3

The grace of the Lord Jesus Christ...

4

...and the love of God and the fellowship
of the Holy Spirit be with you all.
2 Corinthians 13:14

JESUS CHRIST: THE WORD

In the beginning was the Word,
and the Word was with God,
and the Word was God.
John 1:1

In the beginning God created
the heavens and the earth.
Genesis 1:1

*The Bible also refers to Jesus
as "The Word".*

8

*The Word became human and
made his home among us.
He was full of unfailing love
and faithfulness. John 1:14*

**And we have
seen his glory,
the glory of
the Father's
one and
only Son.
John 1:14**

9

Jesus answered, "I am the way and the truth and the life. No one comes to the Father except through me. John 14:6

Follow Jesus.

JESUS CHRIST
GAVE HIS LIFE
FOR US

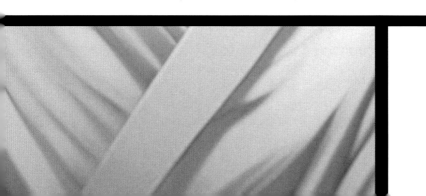

13

For this is how God loved the world: He gave his one and only Son, so that everyone who believes in him will not perish but have eternal life. John 3:16

14

But he (Jesus Christ) was pierced for our rebellion, crushed for our sins. He was beaten so we could be whole. He was whipped so we could be healed.
Isaiah 53:5

15

But thanks be to God, which giveth us the victory through our Lord Jesus Christ. I Corinthians 15:57

16

Victorious through
Christ Jesus.

**JESUS CHRIST
IS ALIVE**

The Son of Man must be given over into the hands of sinful men. He must be nailed to a cross. He will rise again three days later.
Luke 24:7

20

Christ was raised from the dead, and he will never die again. Death no onger has any power over him.
Romans 6:9

21

**WHAT IS
YOUR IDENTITY
IN CHRIST?**

**HOW DOES JESUS
SEE YOU?**

By partnering with Christ,
you are embracing your true purpose
and doing what He created you for.

You are on earth to be
- in your own unique way -
a reflection of Jesus Christ
through your words and actions.

I knew you before I formed you in your mother's womb. Before you were born I set you apart and appointed you as my prophet to the nations. Jeremiah 1:5

Realize that
I am
in my Father,
and you are
in me,
and I am
in you.
John 14:20

25

I am the vine; you are
the branches. If you
remain in me and I in
you, you will bear much
fruit; apart from me you
can do nothing.
If you do not remain
in me, you are
like a branch
that is thrown away
and withers.
John 15:4-6

26

You are the light
of the world.
Matthew 5:14

27

My sheep listen to My voice; I know them, and they follow Me. I give them eternal life, and they will never perish. No one can snatch them out of My hand. My Father who has given them to Me is greater than all. No one can snatch them out of My Father's hand. I and the Father are one. John 10:27-30

I give unto them eternal life; and they shall never perish, neither shall any man pluck them out of my hand. My Father, which gave them me, is greater than all; and no man is able to pluck them out of my Father's hand. John 10:28-29

29

The LORD will make you
the head, not the tail.
Deuteronomy 28:13

**For we are God's workmanship,
created in Christ Jesus to do
good works,
which God prepared
in advance as our way of life.
Ephesians 2:10**

We are Christ's ambassadors;
God is making his appeal
through us. We speak for Christ
when
we plead, "Come back to God!"
2 Corinthians 5:20

32

Jesus Christ, has made us kings and priests to His God and Father. Revelation 1:6

33

**His eyes were as a flame of fire.
Revelation 19:12-15**

*He makes his messengers winds,
his ministers a flaming fire. Psalm 104:4*

34

God raised us up with Christ and seated us with him in the heavenly realms in Christ Jesus. Ephesians 2:6

35

WHAT IS EXPECTED OF YOU?

If you want to partner with Jesus,
you must get to know Him.
Know who He is, what He likes and dislikes.

**Where can you find! this information?
In the bible.**

39

By reading, studying and meditating on bible verses, you will gain a profound understanding of who Jesus Christ is and what He desires.

The bible is also called
The Word of God.

41

**All Scripture is inspired by God and
is useful to teach us what is true and to
make us realize what is wrong in our
lives. It corrects us when we are wrong
and teaches us to do what is right.**
2 Timothy 3:16

For the word of God is alive and active.
Sharper than any double-edged sword,
it penetrates even to dividing soul and
spirit, joints and marrow; it judges
the thoughts and attitudes of the heart.
Hebrews 4:12

Everyone who hears these words of mine and puts them into practice is like a wise man who built his house on the rock. Matthew 7:24

44

Seek the things that are above,
where Christ is, seated
at the right hand of God.

Colossians
3:1

45

Let your light shine before men, that. they may see your good works, and glorify your Father which is in heaven. Matthew 5:16

46

Do you not know that your bodies are temples of the Holy Spirit, who is in you, whom you have received from God? You are not your own; you were bought at a price. Therefore honor God with your bodies.
I Corinthians 6:19-20

47

DON'T WORRY
HAVE FAITH

For God has not given us
a spirit of fear and timidity,
but of power, love,
and self-discipline.
2 Timothy 1:7

51

If God be for us, who can be against us?
Romans 8:31

**Greater is he that is in you,
than he that is in the world.
I John 4:4**

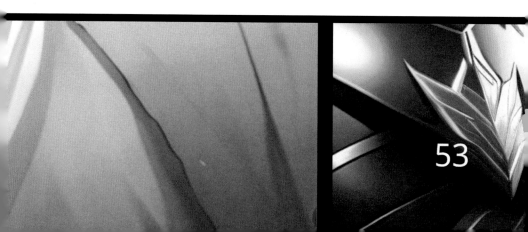

**Blessed are all they
that put their trust in him.
Psalms 2:12**

Behold, the eye of the LORD is upon them
that fear him, upon them that hope
in his mercy; To deliver their soul from
death, and to keep them alive in famine.
Psalms 33:18-19

55

Come to Me, all you who are
weary and burdened, and I will give you
rest. Take My yoke upon you and learn
from Me; for I am gentle and humble
in heart, and you will find rest
for your souls.
Matthew 11:28-29

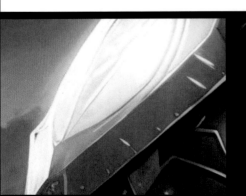

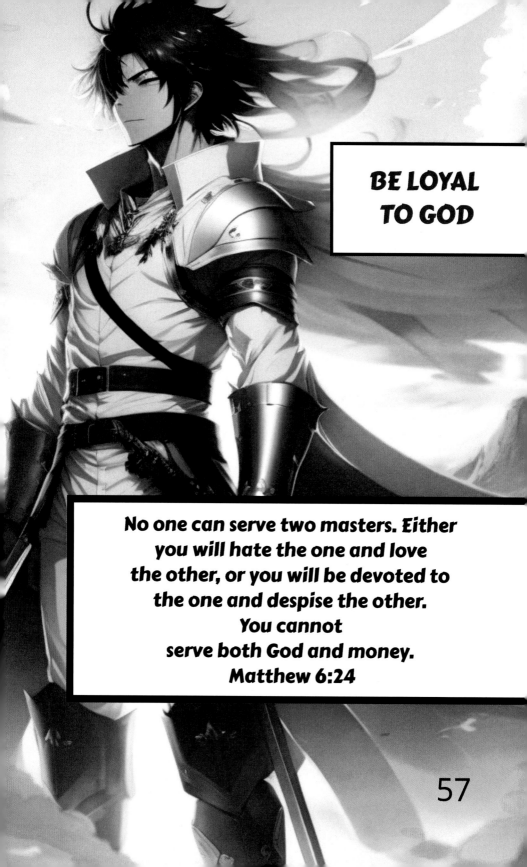

BE LOYAL TO GOD

No one can serve two masters. Either you will hate the one and love the other, or you will be devoted to the one and despise the other. You cannot serve both God and money.
Matthew 6:24

PRAY

Don't worry
about anything;
instead,
pray about everything.
Tell God
what you need,
and thank him
for all he has done.
Philippians 4:6

FORGIVE

Bless those who persecute you. Don't curse them; pray that God will bless them.
Romans 12:14

59

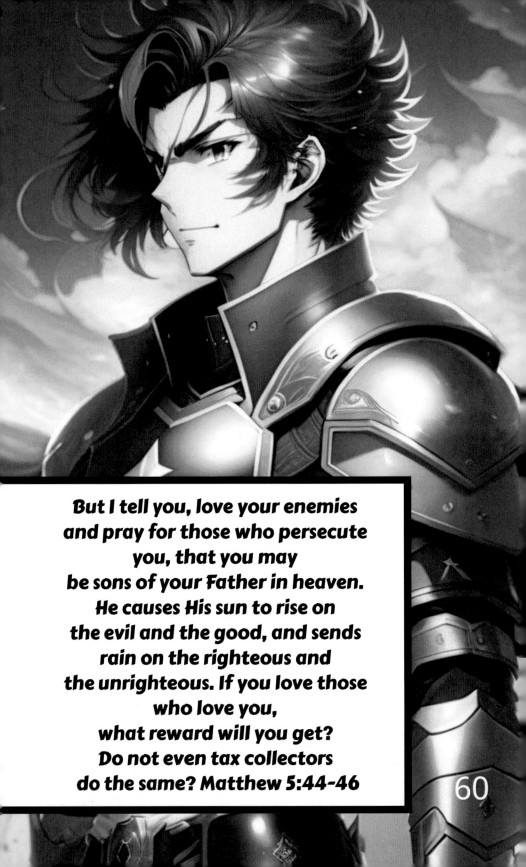

But I tell you, love your enemies and pray for those who persecute you, that you may be sons of your Father in heaven. He causes His sun to rise on the evil and the good, and sends rain on the righteous and the unrighteous. If you love those who love you, what reward will you get? Do not even tax collectors do the same? Matthew 5:44-46

60

BE PATIENT

But they that wait upon the LORD shall renew their strength; they shall mount up with wings as eagles; they shall run, and not be weary; and they shall walk, and not faint. Isaiah 40:31

62

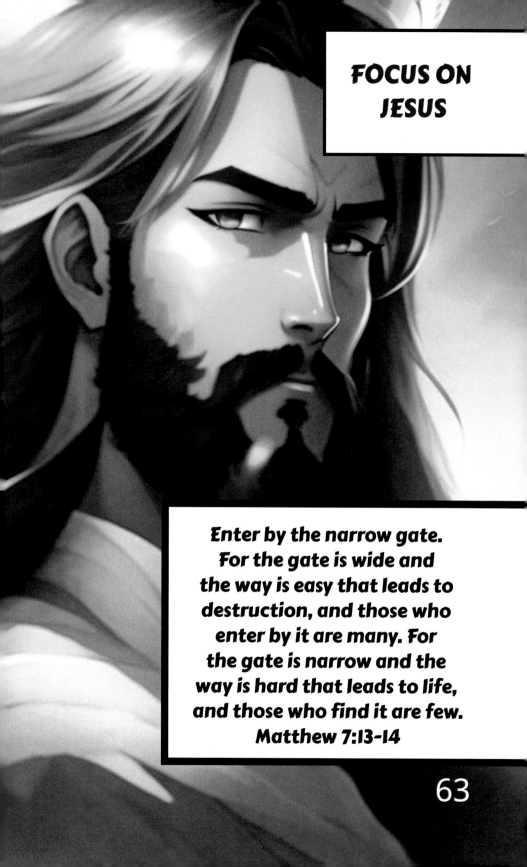

FOCUS ON JESUS

Enter by the narrow gate. For the gate is wide and the way is easy that leads to destruction, and those who enter by it are many. For the gate is narrow and the way is hard that leads to life, and those who find it are few.
Matthew 7:13-14

63

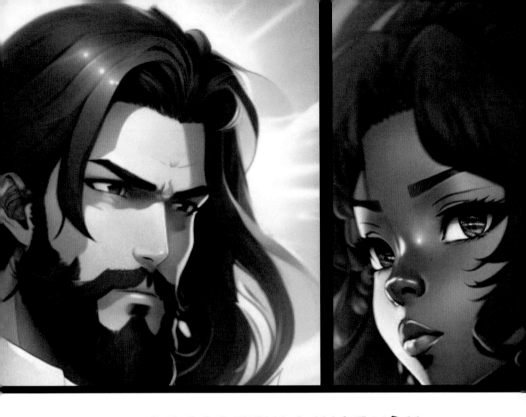

BE CAREFUL WHAT YOU WATCH

Your eye is like a lamp that provides light for your body. When your eye is healthy, your whole body is filled with light. But when your eye is unhealthy, your whole body is filled with darkness. Matthew 6:22-23

BE CAREFUL WHAT YOU SAY
BE CAREFUL WHAT YOU LISTEN TO

I tell you, on the day of judgment people will give account for every careless word they speak.
Matthew 12:36

Avoid all perverse talk; stay away from corrupt speech. Proverbs 4:24

67

Every day become a little
more like Christ.

But the fruit of the Spirit is love, joy,
peace, forbearance, kindness,
goodness, faithfulness, gentleness and
self-control. Galatians 5:22-23

NOT OF THIS WORLD

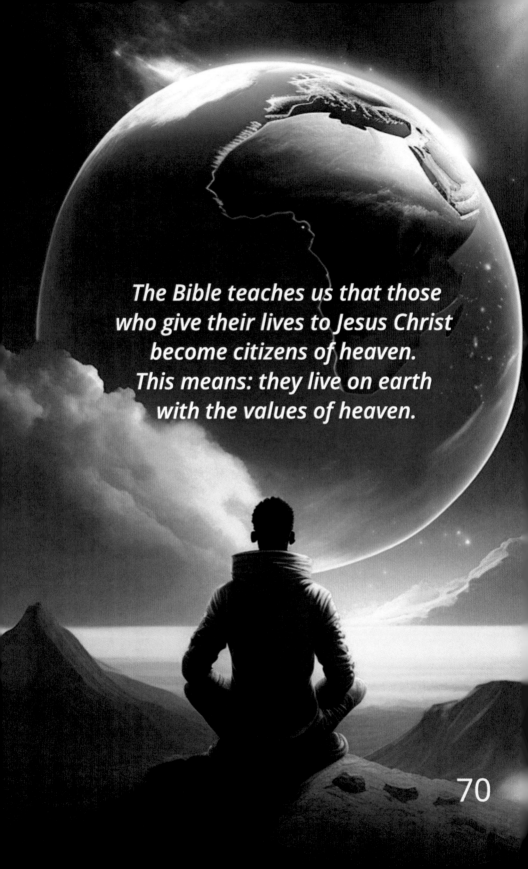

The Bible teaches us that those who give their lives to Jesus Christ become citizens of heaven. This means: they live on earth with the values of heaven.

70

71

He has delivered us from the domain of darkness and transferred us to the kingdom of his beloved Son.
Colossians 1:13

72

73

> For we know that if the tent that
> is our earthly home is destroyed,
> we have a building from God,
> a house not made with hands,
> eternal in the heavens.
> **2 Corinthians 5:1**

But our citizenship is in heaven, and from it we await a Savior, the Lord Jesus Christ, who will transform our lowly body to be like his glorious body, by the power that enables him even to subject all things to himself.
Philippians 3:20-21

76

If ye were of the world, the world would love his own: but because ye are not of the world, but I have chosen you out of the world, therefore the world hateth you. John 15:19

Love not the world, neither
the things that are in the world.
If any man love the world,
the love of the Father is
not in him. I John 2:15

80

And be not conformed to this world: but be ye transformed by the renewing of your mind, that ye may prove what is that good, and acceptable, and perfect, will of God. Romans 12:2

81

They are not of the world, even as I am not of the world.
John 17:16

82

We are here for only a moment,
visitors and strangers in
the land as our ancestors were
before us. Our days on earth
are like a passing shadow, gone
so soon without a trace.
1 Chronicles 29:15

For our citizenship is in heaven, from which we also eagerly wait for the Savior, the Lord Jesus Christ, 21who will transform our lowly body that it may be conformed to His glorious body, according to the working by which He is able even to subdue all things to Himself.
Philippians 3:20-21

I am with you always, even unto the end of the world. Amen.
Matthew 28:20

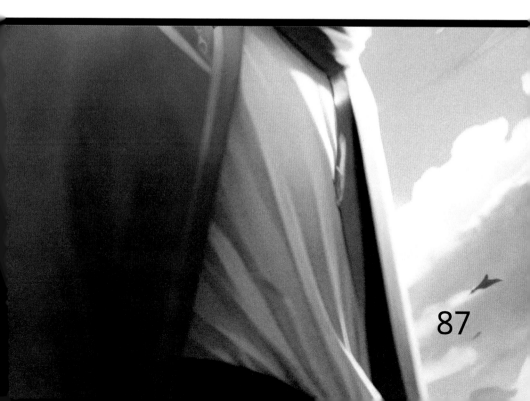

87

Made in the USA
Monee, IL
13 December 2024